COUNTRY

Formal Name: Republic of Haiti (République d'Haïti).

Short Form: Haiti.

Term for Citizens: Haitian(s).

Capital: Port-au-Prince.

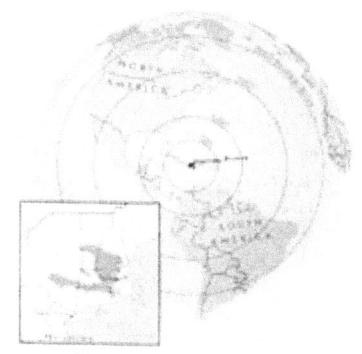

Click to Enlarge Image

Major Cities: Port-au-Prince (917,112 inhabitants), Carrefour (306,074), Delmas (257,247), and Cap-Haïtien (107,026) are Haiti's only cities with more than 100,000 inhabitants.

Independence: January 1, 1804, from France. Haiti was the first modern state governed by people of African descent and the second nation in the Western Hemisphere to achieve independence.

Public Holidays: Haiti celebrates the following public holidays: Independence Day (January 1), Ancestors' Day (January 2), Carnival Monday (variable date in February or March), Mardi Gras (variable date in February or March), Ash Wednesday (variable date in February or March), Good Friday (variable date in March or April, Friday before Easter), Easter (variable date in March or April), Flag Day (May 18), Ascension Day (variable date in May or June), Corpus Christi Day (variable date in May or June), Assumption Day (August 15), Dessalines Day (October 17), All Saints' Day (November 1), All Souls' Day (November 2), and Christmas Day (December 25).

Flag: Haiti's flag consists of two equal horizontal bands, the top blue and the bottom red. Centered is a white rectangle that bears Haiti's coat of arms, which consists of a palm tree and two cannons underscored by the motto "L'UNION FAIT LA FORCE" (Union Makes Strength).

Click to Enlarge Image

HISTORICAL BACKGROUND

Early History: Haiti has a uniquely tragic history. Natural disasters, poverty, racial discord, and political instability have plagued the small country throughout its history. Before the arrival of Europeans, Arawak (also known as Taino) and Carib Indians inhabited the island of Hispaniola. Although researchers debate the total pre-Columbian population (estimates range from 60,000 to 600,000), the detrimental impact of colonization is well documented. Disease and brutal labor practices nearly annihilated the Indian population within 50 years of Columbus's arrival.

Spain ceded the western third of the island of Hispaniola to France in 1697. French authorities quelled the island's buccaneer activity and focused on agricultural growth. Soon, French adventurers began to settle the colony, turning the French portion of the island, renamed Saint-Domingue, into a coffee- and sugar-producing juggernaut. By the 1780s, nearly 40 percent of all the sugar imported by Britain and France and 60 percent of the world's coffee came from the small colony. For a brief time, Saint-Domingue annually produced more exportable wealth than all of continental North America.

As the indigenous population dwindled, African slave labor became vital to Saint-Domingue's economic development. Slaves arrived by the tens of thousands as coffee and sugar production boomed. Under French colonial rule, nearly 800,000 slaves arrived from Africa, accounting for a third of the entire Atlantic slave trade. Many died from disease and the harsh conditions of the sugar and coffee plantations. Statistics show that there was a complete turnover in the slave population every 20 years. Despite these losses, by 1789 slaves outnumbered the free population four-to-one—452,000 slaves in a population of 520,000.

By the mid-eighteenth century, Saint Domingue's society had settled into a rigid hierarchical structure based on skin color, class, and wealth. At the bottom of the social ladder were the African-born plantation slaves; slightly above them were the Creole slaves, who were born in the New World and spoke the French Creole dialect; the two next highest rungs were made up of the mixed-race mulatto slaves and the *affranchis*, or mulatto freedmen, respectively. Whites constituted the top of the social structure but were broadly divided between the lower-ranking shopkeeper and smallholder class (*petits blancs*) and the high-ranking plantation owners, wealthy merchants, and high officials (*grands blancs*).

During the latter eighteenth century, the fabric of Saint-Domingue's hierarchical society began to unravel. Slaves abandoned the plantations in increasing numbers, establishing runaway slave (maroon) communities in remote areas of the colony. The more militant maroon communities posed a threat to the plantations, subjecting them to constant harassment and facilitating slave revolts and mass escapes. Meanwhile, free blacks and mulattoes sought full citizenship and property rights— including the right to own slaves—and arable land for farming. During the 1790s, the dissolution of the Bourbon dynasty by the French Revolution and France's embrace of an egalitarian ethos emboldened Saint-Domingue's free people of color to press for their rights. In 1790 the National Assembly in Paris granted suffrage to landed and tax-paying free blacks. When the white planter-dominated colonial assembly refused to comply, Saint-Domingue became engulfed in violence. The breakdown in civil order prompted numerous slave revolts as well as Spanish and British military intervention. The conflict revolved around a struggle for control of the colony between French republican forces and Creole royalists backed by Spain and Britain. Both sides recruited indigenous armies of black slaves, free blacks, and mulattoes.

Emancipation and Independence: In 1791 Toussaint Louverture emerged as a commander within the rebel army of black slaves led by Georges Biassou and Jean-François. Louverture, an educated former slave who had studied the military campaigns of Julius Caesar, provided the forceful leadership and organizational ability that had been lacking in previous uprisings. Louverture initially allied with Spain in its efforts to capture northern Saint-Domingue but switched his allegiance to France in 1794 when Paris declared the abolition of slavery. He eventually rose to become the commander in chief of all republican forces in Saint-Domingue. From this position, Louverture once again rebelled against the French and attempted to create an autonomous state free of European influence. After deposing the French commissioner, he captured the Spanish port of Santo Domingo in 1800, giving him control of the entire island of Hispaniola.

In October 1801, a break in the Napoleonic Wars enabled France to dispatch a new expedition against Louverture. The rebel general was eventually compelled to surrender to the French after his two top commanders, Jean-Jacques Dessalines and Henry Christophe, switched their allegiance to the French. However, the truce between black Creole and French forces was short-lived. In the summer of 1802, Dessalines, Christophe, and the mulatto general Alexandre Pétion joined forces and launched a new campaign to expel the French. By late 1803, French losses from yellow fever, malaria, and combat exceeded 52,000. The resumption of war in Europe compelled France to withdraw in November 1803. After 300 years of colonial rule, the new nation of Haiti was declared an independent republic. It was only the second nation in the Americas to gain its independence and the first modern state governed by people of African descent.

During the early years of independence, Haiti's cohesion, autonomy, and finances remained precarious. The new "black republic" was diplomatically and economically isolated and faced a continuing threat of foreign intervention. France did not recognize Haitian independence and sought to establish a protectorate over its former colony. The plantation system—the engine of the Haitian economy—lay in ruins after years of warfare. Despite the egalitarianism of the new revolutionary regime, Haitian society remained hierarchical, with deep disparities in wealth between the mixed-race mulatto freedmen and newly emancipated blacks. Following the departure of most of the French Creoles, the mulatto minority took their place as the new elite within Haitian society. Rural laborers resisted efforts by mulatto landowners to rebuild sugar plantations, preferring instead to work the land independently.

Upon independence in 1804, Louverture's lieutenant, Dessalines, became Haiti's first head of state. An autocrat who ruled mainly through force, Dessalines declared himself Emperor Jacques I. His despotic rule, which the mulatto elite resisted, ended with his assassination in October 1806.

Partition: Following the death of Dessalines, a bitter power struggle developed between two of the surviving leaders of the independence movement, Henry Christophe and Alexandre Pétion. A constitutional scheme whereby Christophe and Pétion would jointly govern the country quickly fell apart, leading to a territorial partition that lasted from 1811 to 1820.

Reunification and Annexation of Santo Domingo: In 1820, following the deaths of both Christophe and Pétion, forces from the southern half of Haiti led by General Jean-Pierre Boyer, a mulatto, invaded the north and reunited the country. During his two decades as president, Boyer vigorously defended Haitian sovereignty through a combination of military confrontation and negotiation with the European powers. In 1822 Boyer invaded Santo Domingo, expelling the Spanish and imposing a 22-year occupation of the neighboring nation. Toward the end of his tenure, Boyer negotiated a payment to France of 150 million francs (later reduced to 60 million francs) as indemnity for the loss of the colony. In exchange, France recognized the Republic of Haiti and restored trade relations. Although the indemnity helped secure Haiti's political independence, it imposed a crushing economic burden that weighed heavily on future generations. Boyer held office until his overthrow in 1843 by a conspiracy of reformist mulattoes. In February 1844, a band of Dominican nationalists took the opportunity of Boyer's ouster to attack the Haitian garrison in Santo Domingo and declare an independent Dominican Republic.

Presidential Rule: Throughout the nineteenth century, Haiti's political institutions were subject to the whims of the Haitian head of state. Successive presidents drafted and abolished the nation's constitutions at will, treating the documents as their own personal charters. The Haitian republic itself was suspended from 1849 to 1859 during the rule of "Emperor" Faustin I. Economic stagnation plagued the country, as governments repeatedly subdivided agricultural lands, causing yields to plummet. The indemnity to France also dragged down Haiti's struggling economy. Political solutions rarely overcame the deep-seated hostility between blacks and mulattoes. Elite mulattoes, for the most part, either held the presidency or managed to install puppet black presidents who served their interests.

Coups and assassinations became commonplace. One president died when the presidential palace was blown up, another was hacked to pieces by an angry mob, and a third was poisoned. In the midst of this political chaos, only three Haitian presidents enjoyed relatively stable and effective tenures. General Nicholas Geffrard (1859–67), during a generally peaceful and progressive administration, succeeded in gaining recognition for Haiti from the United States in 1862. Louis Lysius Félicité Salomon (1879–88) implemented populist reforms and established a national bank, telegraph system, and rural school system. Florvil Hyppolite (1889–96) created the Ministry of Public Works, which built much-needed bridges, docks, and public buildings throughout the country.

U.S. Occupation, 1915–34: During most of the nineteenth century, the United States maintained a distant relationship with Haiti. The U.S. government withheld recognition of Haiti until 1862, when wartime necessity compelled it to establish cordial relations with the strategic Caribbean nation. During the early twentieth century, Haiti's chronic political instability, its precarious finances, and the threat of European encroachment provoked numerous brief interventions by the U.S. Navy. In July 1915, civil unrest surrounding the assassination of President Vilbrun Guillaume Sam provided a pretext for intervention. U.S. Marines were dispatched to Haiti, ostensibly to protect U.S. financial interests and citizens. Rather than withdrawing after a show of "gunboat diplomacy," as had previously been the case, the U.S. military came to stay in 1915. Marines seized control of the country, disbanding the Haitian military and installing Phillippe Sudre Dartiguenave, a mulatto, as president (1915–22). In 1916 the United States expanded its occupation to the entire island of Hispaniola when it intervened in the neighboring Dominican Republic. During its nearly two-decade occupation, the United States amended the Haitian constitution, stabilized the economy, and made improvements in infrastructure. U.S. Marines also trained a new Haitian National Guard (Garde d'Haïti), a security unit that harassed and even killed opponents of the occupation.

New Independence: In 1930 the United States allowed Haiti to resume free elections. The president-elect, Sténio Vincent (1930–41), was a former senator with populist tendencies, and his election set Haiti on the path to reestablishing its autonomy. Vincent engaged in an ambitious program of infrastructure improvement, while insisting that the U.S. Marines end their active occupation. As a show of nationalism, he delivered his state addresses in Creole, rather than in French. Like many of his predecessors, however, Vincent also resorted to using the presidency to increase his own wealth and power. In 1935 he pushed through the Haitian Congress a new constitution that allowed the president to disband the legislature and reorganize the judiciary. Ultimately, Vincent succeeded in reestablishing Haiti's independence, but he also strengthened the country's legacy of dictatorial leadership.

After the ineffective administration of Élie Lescot (1941–45), which installed mulattoes in virtually every post of the government, black voters turned out en masse and elected a sympathetic National Assembly. Additionally, after years of mulatto rule, the 1946 presidential election, often referred to as the Revolution of 1946, was contested by three black candidates. Dumarsais Estimé (1946–50) won the election, garnering especially strong support from the emerging middle class of blacks in the northern region of the country. Colonel Paul Magloire followed Estimé in 1950 and held the presidency for six corrupt, if stable, years.

The Duvalier Era: François Duvalier (1957–71) won a suspiciously large victory in the presidential election of 1957. Duvalier came from a modest black family in Port-au-Prince. His platform consisted of pro-black nationalism, strong support from the military, and state acceptance of the voodoo religion. The army disqualified Duvalier's most popular rival, Daniel Fignolé, and likely tampered with ballots. Amidst the controversy, Duvalier officially assumed the presidency in 1957, backed by a majority in both houses of the legislature.

As a candidate for office, Duvalier had been known as "Papa Doc" because of his paternalistic concern for poor and sick Haitians. During his 14-year reign, however, Duvalier focused more on controlling his people than caring for them. His dictatorial methods were harsh even by Haiti's standards. In 1961 he discarded the bicameral legislature in favor of a unicameral one and then secured for himself the title of president for life. In order to control the military, Duvalier frequently shuffled the leadership, bringing young black soldiers to command positions until they too became threatening to the administration. Duvalier also created the Presidential Guard and the Volunteers for National Security (Volontaires de la Sécurité Nationale—VSN), or *makout* as they were known, for the express purpose of averting attempted coups. The VSN functioned as a secret paramilitary group, using blackmail and terror to control Haiti's citizenry.

Largely through his brutal tactics, Duvalier held the presidency until his natural death in 1971. His son, Jean-Claude (1971–86), assumed leadership of Haiti at the age of 19. After initially deferring to his ambitious mother, Jean-Claude, referred to as "Baby Doc," adopted many of his father's leadership tactics. He lived lavishly, siphoning off funds from the governmentally controlled tobacco industry, while Haiti descended further into poverty. The administration relied heavily on intimidation to maintain power. A visit from Pope John Paul II on March 9, 1983, saw the pope echoing the people's cries for improved access to food, water, education, and employment. It proved to be the beginning of the end for Jean-Claude. On February 7, 1986, Haitian citizens revolted against the corruption-rife administration. Threatened by rioting crowds and pressured by the United States, Duvalier gave up the presidency and went into exile in France.

Jean-Bertrand Aristide and the Struggle for Democracy: Duvalier had hastily named a National Council of Government (Conseil National de Gouvernement—CNG) to serve as an interim government. Although the CNG initially dismantled some vestiges of the Duvalier era, it too eventually slipped into the mode of repressive governance. Brigadier General Prosper Avril assumed the presidency in September 1988 and governed for two tumultuous years before a wave of assassinations and widespread public protests led to his resignation in March 1990. Following Avril's departure, an independent Permanent Electoral Council announced a presidential election for December 16, 1990.

Despite widespread violence, Haiti's presidential election of December 1990 proved to be a landmark event. International observers declared the election to be free and fair. Outspoken anti-Duvalierist and former Roman Catholic priest Jean-Bertrand Aristide won a landslide victory with 67 percent of the vote. A fiery populist who elicited fanatical support from the poorest sectors of Haitian society, Aristide pledged to rid Haiti of the ethnic, racial, and economic hierarchy that had defined the country. He became a polarizing figure opposed by much of the country's elite and the armed forces. During his first months in office, Aristide circumscribed the military's power by establishing a separate presidential security force, closing military facilities, and reducing the armed forces budget. He also antagonized the economic elite by collecting back taxes and by appearing to endorse violence against his opponents. After only seven months in office, Aristide was ousted by a military coup on September 29, 1991. A junta led by Brigadier General Raoul Cédras seized control of the government. The military government engaged in systematic repression of dissidents and Aristide supporters, including numerous extrajudicial killings. In the midst of severe repression and a worsening of already dire economic conditions, tens of thousands of Haitians attempted to flee to Florida by boat. The U.S. Coast Guard rescued more than 40,000 Haitians at sea during 1991 and 1992. Thousands more may have perished at sea. The United States condemned the coup and pledged to see Aristide restored to office. Additionally, the United Nations (UN) Security Council refused to recognize Haiti's new leaders and imposed multilateral economic sanctions.

In mid-1994, after two and a half years of economic sanctions, the UN Security Council approved the deployment of a multinational force to restore civilian authority in Haiti. With a United States-led military invasion looming, the junta agreed to step down in return for amnesty for themselves and the rest of the army. On September 9, 1994, U.S. troops entered Haiti unopposed, restoring Aristide to office. Aristide's principal achievement during the remainder of his term was the abolition of the Haitian army and its replacement by the United States-trained Haitian National Police.

Political Chaos: In 1995 Aristide completed his term, and Haiti had its first transition between two democratically elected presidents. Constitutionally barred from a consecutive term, Aristide picked his political ally and former prime minister, René Préval, as his successor. Préval's tenure was characterized by partisan rancor and executive-legislative deadlock. Elections in 1997 for one-third of the Senate and communal assemblies were plagued with allegations of fraud and were not certified by international observers. During a prolonged constitutional crisis, the Préval government was unable to organize a second round of local and parliamentary elections due in late 1998. In January 1999, Préval dismissed legislators whose terms had expired—the entire Chamber of Deputies and all but nine members of the Senate—and governed by presidential decree. When legislative, local, and municipal elections were finally held in May 2000, Aristide and Préval reportedly pressed the Provisional Electoral Council to exclude nearly a quarter of the votes cast, using a formula that violated two articles of Haiti's constitution. In the summer of 2000, in response to credible evidence of government corruption, election fraud, and widespread human rights violations, Haiti's foreign donors suspended all development assistance. The presidential election held in November 2000 was boycotted by the opposition and the Organization of American States (OAS) observer mission, which considered the results to be heavily tainted by fraud. So low was confidence in Haiti's government that only 5 to 15 percent of the electorate is believed to have voted. The disputed election returned Aristide to office by a wide margin.

Aristide's second tenure as president (2001–4) saw an intensification of political violence, an economic recession, and a breakdown of government institutions and the rule of law. Haiti's economy experienced a sharp recession following the cutoff of foreign aid. Beginning in 2001, real gross domestic product (GDP) growth turned negative—a trend that would continue for the next three years. Political violence intensified as pro- and anti-Aristide militants battled in the streets. In December 2001, 30 armed men attempted to seize the National Palace in an apparent coup attempt. The government blamed former army officers for the failed raid. In retaliation, throughout 2002 and 2003 the government orchestrated attacks on opposition demonstrations by police and government-supported gangs known as *chimères*. In turn, the opposition Democratic Convergence alliance called for Aristide's removal and announced plans for a transitional government. In March 2003, a high-level joint delegation of the OAS and Caribbean Community and Common Market (Caricom) presented specific demands to President Aristide to restore public security and create the confidence necessary to move toward elections. However, little in the way of progress was achieved. In January 2004, during celebrations of the Haitian bicentennial, crowds frustrated by the government's ineffectiveness rioted in the city of Cap Haïtien. The rioting quickly spread across the country, escalating into a full-scale rebellion when former members of the armed forces, the police, and gang members joined the fray. By late February 2004, armed rebels demanding Aristide's ouster controlled many of the country's towns and were closing in on the capital of Port au Prince. Unable to quell the rebellion, and facing an imminent threat to his safety, Aristide resigned the presidency in late February and was airlifted out of the country by U.S. armed forces. Boniface Alexandre, president of Haiti's Supreme Court, assumed the presidency in accordance with the constitution.

Responding to an emerging humanitarian crisis, a United States-led Multilateral Interim Force made up of troops from the United States, Canada, France, and Chile, was dispatched to secure Haiti's ports and restore the flow of food and medical supplies into the country. In April 2004, the UN Security Council adopted Resolution 1542, creating the UN Stability Mission in Haiti (MINUSTAH). The Stability Mission was authorized at 6,700 troops and 1,622 civilian police. Brazil contributed the largest contingent of troops to MINUSTAH.

During 2004 and 2005, MINUSTAH and the interim Haitian government struggled to restore law and order and lay the groundwork for national elections. After several postponements, the first round of elections for president and the National Assembly took place on February 7, 2006. Turnout was estimated at approximately 60 percent of registered voters. Former President Préval won the presidential contest with 51.15 percent of the vote. The election was marred by controversy when the Electoral Council posted partial results indicating that Préval had not won a majority of the votes cast. However, following demonstrations in Haiti and expressions of concern by the international community, the Electoral Council reversed its decision to count large numbers of blank ballots and declared Préval the first-round winner.

In the spring of 2006, Haiti's future under a second Préval administration remained uncertain. The new administration faced numerous challenges, including the need to rein in endemic criminality and gang violence, restore public services, and foster economic growth and poverty reduction. Whether Haiti's current generation of political leaders would be able to negotiate in good faith and reach political solutions to national problems remained to be seen.

GEOGRAPHY

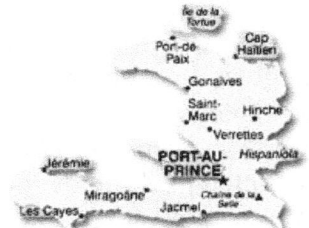

Click to Enlarge Image

Location: Haiti occupies the western third of the island of Hispaniola, which is situated in the Caribbean between Cuba and Puerto Rico. The Dominican Republic occupies the remainder of the island. The Atlantic Ocean borders Haiti's northern shores, while the Caribbean Sea is to the west and south. The Windward Passage separates Haiti from Cuba, which lies about 80 kilometers to the northwest.

Size: Haiti occupies 27,750 square kilometers of land, making it approximately the same size as the state of Maryland.

Land Boundaries: Haiti shares a 360-kilometer border with the Dominican Republic to the east.

Disputed Territory: Traditional conflicts with the Dominican Republic over the border have been largely settled. The Protocol of Revision of 1936 set the present border.

Length of Coastline: Because of its horseshoe shape, Haiti has a disproportionately long coastline. In all, Haiti's coastline stretches 1,771 kilometers, with prominent peninsulas in both the north and the south.

Maritime Claims: Haiti claims a territorial sea of 12 nautical miles, a contiguous zone of 24 nautical miles, an exclusive economic zone of 200 nautical miles, and a continental shelf to the depth of exploitation.

Topography: Haiti occupies the mountainous portion of the island of Hispaniola. Its land area includes numerous small islands as well as four large islands: Île de la Gonâve to the west, Île de la Tortue off the north coast, and Île à Vache and Grande Cayemite, situated, respectively, south and north of the southern peninsula. Five mountain ranges dominate Haiti's landscape and divide the country into three regions—northern, central, and southern. Slopes of more than a 20 percent grade cover nearly two-thirds of the country. Plains constitute only about 20 percent of Haiti's land, making cultivation difficult.

The northern region has the country's largest coastal plain, the Plaine du Nord, which covers an area of 2,000 square kilometers. The north's major mountain range, the Massif du Nord, buttresses this plain. The central region consists of the Central Plateau, which covers an area of more than 2,500 square kilometers, as well as two smaller plains and three mountain ranges. The Guayamouc River splits the Central Plateau and provides some of the country's most fertile soil. Haiti's southern region contains a series of small coastal plains as well as the mountains of the Massif de la Selle. It encompasses both Haiti's highest point—Montagne Terrible, 2,684 meters—and the Plaine du Cul-de-Sac, which is a natural depression 12 kilometers wide and 32 kilometers wide.

Principal Rivers: Haiti's rivers often overflow during the rainy season and conversely slow to a trickle during the dry season. Five rivers provide most of the country's catchment: the Artibonite, Grand-Anse, L'Estère, Trois Rivières, and Cavaillon. The Artibonite is the country's dominant drainage system and was dammed in 1956 to create Lac de Péligre. The Libon River, which feeds into the Artibonite, forms part of Haiti's border with the Dominican Republic and also provides the country with most of its electricity—through the Péligre Dam, Haiti's major hydroelectric facilty. In addition to rivers, the country's mountainous terrain also has created a series of short and swift streams, running between mountain ridges.

Climate: Haiti has a tropical climate with distinct dry and wet seasons—the former from December to February and the latter between April and November. The eastern region of the country is the exception to the tropical climate. Mountains block trade winds there, creating a semiarid climate. Rainfall varies considerably. In the northwest, rainfall averages about 300 millimeters annually while the southwestern mountains receive more than 3,000 millimeters of rain each year. In terms of temperature, the coastal regions enjoy averages near 27° C with only minor variations throughout the year. By contrast, the mountainous regions regularly experience fronts during the winter months. Because of the northeast trade winds, the entire country periodically faces extreme weather conditions. Haitians must contend with hurricanes, droughts, floods, and other natural disasters.

Natural Resources: Haiti has limited natural resources because of its relatively small land area and environmental degradation. Of Haiti's natural resources, wood may be the most vital. Mangrove forests cover about 180 square kilometers of Haiti's coastal areas. This valuable wood resource, however, is in decline as a result of overuse. In addition to wood, Haiti has some mineral deposits, including bauxite, copper, gold, and lignite. Known deposits of high-grade calcium carbonate exist but have yet to be mined. Haiti has numerous sites where construction materials—such as gravel, limestone, clay, and sand—can be gathered. Haiti's rivers give the country access to hydropower, but the fluctuating water volumes make harnessing this resource difficult.

Land Use: By agronomic standards, the majority of Haiti's land (63 percent) is too steep for agricultural production, and only about 28 percent is considered arable. Despite this fact, nearly 80 percent of the country's area functions, at least temporarily, as agricultural land. These less than ideal conditions make yields low and stability difficult. Only 11.5 percent of the land is used for permanent crops. Irrigation is limited, and the government's recent commitment to irrigating 40,000 hectares within five years was called off with only 5,600 hectares improved. Mountains take up a significant portion of the country, and concentrated urban areas house most of the country's population.

Environmental Factors: Haiti faces a severe deforestation problem. In 1923 forests covered nearly 60 percent of the country; today they cover less than 2 percent. Until recently the government had done little to combat this problem. Because most Haitians still depend on wood and charcoal as their primary fuel source, energy alternatives are needed to save the forests. The 15-year Environment Action Plan, authorized in 1999, proposed to stop deforestation by developing alternative fuel sources. So far, however, political instability and lack of funding have limited the impact of this reform effort. Deforestation has led to soil erosion, which has decreased agricultural yields and resulted in deadly landslides. Urban environments suffer from a lack of sanitation. Vast slum areas, especially in the capital, Port-au-Prince, are filled with people living in squalid, unsanitary conditions.

Time Zone: Haiti operates five hours behind Greenwich Mean Time (GMT).

SOCIETY

Population: In 2006 Haiti had an estimated population of 8.3 million, with an annual growth rate of about 2.3 percent. Haiti is the western hemisphere's second most densely populated country (248 persons per square kilometer), trailing only Barbados. About 1.5 million citizens live in the capital and its surrounding districts. Most of the population, however, lives in small cities. In total, Haiti has only four cities with more than 100,000 residents. All population growth has come from childbearing, as Haiti's net migration rate stands at –1.3 migrants per 1,000 population. Population statistics remain difficult to gather because of widespread emigration and the periodic exodus of political refugees in the midst of regime change. Thousands of Haitians in recent years have attempted to reach the shores of the United States, often on unseaworthy vessels.

Demography: Haiti has extremely low life expectancy—about 53 years in 2006 (51.9 years for males and 54.6 years for females). Haiti had an estimated birthrate of 36.4 births per 1,000 population and a death rate of 12.2 deaths per 1,000 population in 2006. Haiti's death rate ranks as the worst in the western hemisphere, as does its 2006 infant mortality rate of nearly 72 deaths per 1,000 live births. In terms of gender, slightly more boys than girls are born in Haiti (1.03 males per female), but because of war, working hardships, and sickness, the total population has fewer males (0.97 males per female) than females. Haitian women have an average of 4.9 children. Most of Haiti's population is under the age of 65. The country's median age is 18. About 42 percent of the population is 14 or younger; 54 percent is 15 to 64 years of age; and 3 percent is 65 and older.

Ethnic Groups and Languages: Nearly all of Haiti's population (95 percent) is of African ancestry. The remaining 5 percent of the population is mulatto or white. The origin of the black population in Haiti can be traced back to the colonial slave trade, when Haiti's thriving sugar plantations needed thousands of slave laborers. French and Creole are Haiti's official languages.

Religion: About 80 percent of Haitians belong to the Roman Catholic faith. Many, however, mix Catholicism with traditional voodoo practices. Roughly half the population still practices voodoo. About 16 percent of the population identifies itself as Protestant, with the Baptist denomination being the largest.

Education and Literacy: Education standards in Haiti are extremely low. Haiti's literacy rate of about 53 percent (55 percent for males and 51 percent for females) falls well below the 90 percent average literacy rate for Latin American and Caribbean countries. Under President Aristide, some improvements have occurred. In 1997 the government passed a 10-year education plan, with the goal of universal access to quality schools. The national education budget increased from 9 percent of the national budget in 1997 to 22 percent in 2000, which paid for programs to provide school lunches, uniforms, and bus transportation. Additionally, in 2002 the government began a literacy campaign, facilitated by 30,000 literacy monitors and the distribution of 700,000 literacy manuals. Overall, school attendance rose from 20 percent in 1994 to 64 percent in 2000. Even with these improvements, however, the country still faces severe shortages in educational supplies and qualified teachers, and the rural population remains vastly underrepresented in the country's classrooms. Currently, most Haitian schools are private rather than state-funded. International private schools (run by Canada, France, or the United States) and church-run schools educate 90 percent of students.

Health: Deficient sanitation systems, poor nutrition, and inadequate health services have pushed Haiti to the bottom of the World Bank's rankings of health indicators. According to the United Nations World Food Programme, 80 percent of Haiti's population lives below the poverty line. Consequently, malnutrition is a significant problem. Half the population can be categorized as "food insecure," and half of all Haitian children are undersized as a result of malnutrition. Less than half the population has access to clean drinking water, a rate that compares poorly even with other less-developed nations. Haiti's healthy life expectancy at birth is only 44 years. The World Health Organization (WHO) estimates that only 43 percent of the target population receives the recommended immunizations.

In terms of health care spending, Haiti ranks last in the western hemisphere. Economic instability has limited any growth in this area. Per capita, Haiti spends about US$83 annually on health care. There are 25 physicians and 11 nurses per 100,000 population. Only one-fourth of births are attended by a skilled health professional. Most rural areas have no access to health care, making residents susceptible to otherwise treatable diseases. In 2003, for example, the WHO confirmed an outbreak of typhoid fever in Haiti that, because of a lack of access to doctors and safe water, led to dozens of deaths.

Haiti has the highest incidence of human immunodeficiency virus/acquired immune deficiency syndrome (HIV/AIDS) outside of Africa. Sex tourism and lack of health education led to the beginning of the epidemic in the early 1980s. Estimates vary, but the United Nations projects the national prevalence rate to be 4.5 percent of the population. Other estimates place the rate as high as 12 percent in the urban population and 5 percent in rural regions. Annually, 5,000 Haitian babies are born infected with the AIDS virus. The disease causes a fifth of all infant deaths and has orphaned 200,000 children.

Welfare: In addition to being the one of the world's most densely populated countries, Haiti is also one of the poorest. The annual per capita income is about US$450, and most of the population (60 percent) faces underemployment. In recent decades, working and living conditions have been so poor that emigration, often by any means possible, has become a popular avenue of escape. About one out of every eight Haitians presently lives outside the country's borders.

The international community has donated heavily to the development of Haiti. Programs to feed, educate, and employ Haitians are funded by various international organizations. Since 1973, the United States has been Haiti's largest donor. Between 1995 and 2003, the United States contributed more than US$850 million to Haiti's development. It also pledged, in 2004, an additional US$230 million in aid through 2006. Although monetary aid has temporarily eased suffering in Haiti, it has failed to significantly alter Haiti's developmental trajectory in the past.

Haiti has an underfunded and largely ineffective social insurance program. Employers are responsible for contributing between 2 and 6 percent of their employees' annual incomes to the social insurance fund. Because most Haitians do not have regular employers, however, this program neglects a large portion of the population. With similar limitations, Haiti has benefits for injured workers, the disabled, and pregnant women.

ECONOMY

Overview: Haiti's economy remains the least developed in the western hemisphere. The potential for economic growth is stymied by political instability, lack of infrastructure, and severe deforestation and soil erosion. Income distribution is highly skewed, and poverty is widespread (about 80 percent of the population lives below the poverty line). Job opportunities are extremely limited. Only one in 50 Haitians has a steady wage-earning job. Rising poverty in Haiti is directly linked to long periods of economic stagnation. Additionally, the country has had the highest rate of inflation among all Caribbean countries.

Gross Domestic Product (GDP): In 2005 Haiti had an estimated GDP of US$4.3 billion (US$12.9 billion in terms of purchasing power parity). Haiti's estimated per capita GDP of US$1,600 in terms of purchasing power parity ranks last in the western hemisphere and 193rd in the world. After experiencing –3.5 percent real GDP contraction in 2004, Haiti's economy saw a modest recovery in 2005, with real GDP growing by 1.5 percent.

Government Budget: During 2005 government expenditures were estimated to be US$600.8 million and revenues, about US$400 million. The government relies heavily on international economic assistance for fiscal sustainability.

Inflation: Purchasing power in Haiti has fluctuated dramatically throughout the past 15 years. Rising fuel prices and weak domestic demand, coupled with political instability, have produced nearly uncontrollable inflation at times. In 1994 the inflation rate reached 40 percent before an austerity policy and an influx of foreign aid brought it back under control. The inflation rate fell to a manageable 8.7 percent in 1999. However, exchange rate depreciation again pushed inflation to 40 percent in 2003. The inflation rate was about 22 percent in 2004 and an estimated 15 percent in 2005.

Agriculture, Forestry, and Fishing: Although many Haitians make their living through subsistence farming, Haiti also has an agricultural export sector. Agriculture, together with forestry and fishing, accounts for about one-quarter (28 percent in 2004) of Haiti's annual gross domestic product and employs about two-thirds (66 percent in 2004) of the labor force. However, expansion has been difficult because mountains cover much of the countryside and limit the land available for cultivation. Of the total arable land of 550,000 hectares, 125,000 hectares are suited for irrigation, and of those only 75,000 hectares actually have been improved with irrigation. Haiti's dominant cash crops include coffee, mangoes, and cocoa. Haiti has decreased its production of sugarcane, traditionally an important cash crop, because of declining prices and fierce international competition. Because Haiti's forests have thinned dramatically, timber exports have declined. Roundwood removals annually total about 1,000 kilograms. Haiti also has a small fishing industry. Annual catches in recent years have totaled about 5,000 tons.

Mining and Minerals: Haiti has a small mining industry, extracting minerals worth approximately US$13 million annually. Bauxite, copper, calcium carbonate, gold, and marble are the most extensively mined minerals in Haiti.

Industry and Manufacturing: In 2004 industry accounted for about 20 percent of the gross domestic product (GDP), and less than 10 percent of the labor force worked in industrial production. As a portion of the GDP, the manufacturing sector has contracted since the 1980s. The United Nations embargo of 1994 put out of work most of the 80,000 workers in the assembly sector. Additionally, the years of military rule following the presidential coup in 1991 resulted in the closure of most of Haiti's offshore assembly plants in the free zones surrounding Port-au-Prince. When President Aristide returned to Haiti, some improvements did occur in the manufacturing sector. Haiti's cheap labor brought some textile and garment assembly work back to the island in the late 1990s. However, these gains ultimately were undercut by international competition.

The leading industries in Haiti produce beverages, butter, cement, detergent, edible oils, flour, refined sugar, soap, and textiles. Growth in both manufacturing and industry as a whole has been slowed by a lack of capital investment. Grants from the United States and other countries have targeted this problem, but without much success. Private home building and construction appear to be one subsector with positive prospects for growth.

Energy: Haiti uses very little energy, about 250 kilograms of oil equivalent per head per year. In 2003 Haiti produced 546 million kilowatt-hours of electricity while consuming 508 million kilowatt-hours. Most of the country's energy comes from burning wood. Haiti imports oil and consumes about 11,800 barrels per day, as of 2003. The Péligre Dam, the country's largest, provides the capital city of Port-au-Prince with energy. Thermal plants provide electricity to the rest of the country. Traditionally, the supply of electricity has been sporadic and prone to shortages—even with the country's low demand. Mismanagement by the state has offset more than US$100 million in foreign investment targeted at improving Haiti's energy infrastructure. Businesses have resorted to securing back-up power sources to deal with the regular outages. The potential for greater hydropower exists, should Haiti have the desire and means to develop it. The government controls oil and gas prices, insulating Haitians, to an extent, from international price fluctuations.

Services: Haiti's services sector made up 52 percent of the country's gross domestic product in 2004 and employed 25 percent of the labor force. According to World Bank statistics, the services sector is one of the only sectors of Haiti's economy that sustained steady, if modest, growth throughout the 1990s.

Banking and Finance: Lack of a stable and trustworthy banking system has impeded Haiti's economic development. Banks in Haiti have collapsed on a regular basis. Most Haitians do not have access to loans of any sort. When reelected in 2000, President Aristide promised to remedy this situation but instead introduced a non-sustainable plan of "cooperatives" that guaranteed investors a 10 percent rate of return. By 2000 the cooperatives had crumbled, and Haitians collectively had lost more than US$200 million in savings.

Haiti's central bank, the Banque de la République d'Haïti, oversees 10 commercial banks and two foreign banks operating in the country. Most banking takes place in the capital city of Port-au-Prince. The United Nations and the International Monetary Fund have led efforts to diversify and expand the finance sector, making credit more available to rural populations. In 2002 the Canadian International Development Agency led a training program for Haitian Credit Unions. Haiti has no stock exchange.

Tourism: Not surprisingly, tourism in Haiti has suffered from the country's political upheaval. Inadequate infrastructure also has limited visitors to the island. In the 1970s and 1980s, however, tourism was an important industry, drawing an average of 150,000 visitors annually. Following the 1991 coup, tourism has recovered slowly. The Caribbean Tourism Organization (CTO) has joined the Haitian government in efforts to restore the island's image as a tourist destination. In 2001, 141,000 foreigners visited Haiti. Most came from the United States. Further improvements in hotels, restaurants, and other infrastructure still are needed to make tourism a major industry for Haiti.

Labor: Most Haitians do not have formal jobs. Unemployment and underemployment are rampant. Some estimates suggest that two-thirds of the country's 3.6 million workers are without consistent work. Many Haitians survive through subsistence farming rather than looking for jobs in the overcrowded urban areas. Legal protection does exist for those Haitians employed in the formal sector. Workers have the right of association and collective bargaining. Additionally, the labor code protects workers' unions from recrimination by employers. The country's minimum wage is 70 gourdes per day, equivalent to about US$1.70.

In addition to high unemployment, Haiti also lacks the skilled labor necessary to expand its economy. A brain drain has occurred, and many of the country's skilled workers leave Haiti for better economic opportunities abroad. Annually, thousands of Haitians cross the border to work in the factories of the Dominican Republic. The income they send back to Haiti is significant. Beyond the island of Hispaniola, political turmoil has resulted in many of Haiti's most valuable workers emigrating to the United States and Canada. The 500,000 Haitians living in New York City and the 380,000 in Miami represent a loss of training and expertise that Haiti has been unable to replace.

Foreign Economic Relations: The World Economic Forum ranked Haiti last in its 2003 Global Competitiveness Report. Thus, Haiti's role in the global economy often has been confined to receiving foreign aid. The United States has been the leading donor to development in Haiti and plays a vital role in Haiti's economy. Haiti maintains active membership in a variety of multinational economic organizations, including the International Coffee Organization, Latin American Economic System, and Caribbean Community and Common Market. Haiti also is a signatory to the Cotonou Convention—an economic community seeking to foster trade among African, Caribbean, and Pacific countries.

Imports: Haitian imports totaled an estimated US$1.5 billion in 2005. About 35 percent of imports came from the United States. Other significant sources of imports that year included the Netherlands Antilles, Malaysia, and Colombia. Haiti's primary import items are food, fuels (including oil), machinery, and manufactured goods.

Exports: In 2005 Haiti's exports totaled an estimated US$391 million. More than 80 percent of that revenue came from exports to the United States. Other major export partners in 2005 included the Dominican Republic and Canada. Assembled manufactures, coffee, edible oils, cocoa, and mangoes compose the majority of Haiti's exports.

Trade Balance: Haiti annually has a large trade deficit. In 2005 the country had an estimated trade deficit of about US$1.1 billion.

Balance of Payments: In 2003 Haiti's balance of payments was negative US$4.6 million. Haiti's large trade deficit is partially offset by transfers received, including international aid.

External Debt: Haiti's total external debt surpasses US$1 billion. In 2005 it reached an estimated US$1.3 billion. Following the promising democratic election of Aristide in December 1990, many international creditors responded by canceling significant amounts of Haiti's debt, bringing the total down to US$777 million in 1991. However, new borrowing during the 1990s swelled the debt to more than US$1 billion.

Foreign Investment: Haiti has received very little foreign investment over the past 20 years. Development aid and loans have been the only consistent source of outside capital. In order to encourage foreign investment, in 2004 the interim government approved a three-year "tax holiday" for all foreign businesses that invest in Haiti.

Foreign Aid: Between 1999 and 2004, Haiti's foreign benefactors—the United States, the European Union, the Inter-American Development Bank and the World Bank—jointly suspended aid disbursements in response to evidence of systematic electoral fraud and the failure of the Haitian government to implement accountability measures. Aid was restored in July 2004 after an interim administration was named. Haiti was scheduled to receive more than US$1 billion in pledged aid for 2005 and 2006. The United States pledged US$230 million in aid through fiscal year 2006.

Currency and Exchange Rate: The Haitian currency is the gourde (HTG). In 2005 the exchange rate averaged 40.4 gourdes per US$1. The rate in early May 2006 was 39.65 gourdes per US$1.

Fiscal Year: The Haitian fiscal year begins on October 1 and ends on September 30.

TRANSPORTATION AND TELECOMMUNICATIONS

Overview: Public transportation, as it is understood in the United States, does not exist in Haiti. Most Haitians travel by private car, by bicycle, or on foot. There are about 36 vehicles per 1,000 inhabitants. The road system consists mainly of unmarked and unpaved roads. Local knowledge is necessary to traverse the country. Airports and ports serve the major urban areas.

Roads: Haiti's road system is plagued by insufficient funding and a harsh climate. Seasonal torrential rains ravage the roads that are in place. The United States built much of the road network during the U.S. occupation (1915–34), and thus many stretches need extensive maintenance. Many of the country's bridges are no longer passable. Because road construction has been largely haphazard, no accurate mapping exists of Haiti's road network. At last count (1999), the country had 1,011 kilometers of paved roads and 3,149 kilometers of unpaved roads. Most paved roads surround and service Port-au-Prince, where about 85 percent of the country's traffic is reported to be. Traffic congestion can be extreme in urban areas.

No formal licensing or training program exists for Haitian drivers. Speed limits are posted on some roads, but the police rarely have the manpower to enforce them. Most roads do not have marked lanes or signs indicating the direction of traffic. Old and poorly serviced vehicles lead to frequent traffic accidents and blockages.

Railroads: Haiti has only a small system of privately owned railroad tracks serving the port regions of the country.

Ports: Port-au-Prince serves as Haiti's primary port for both cargo and passenger ships. The government currently owns and operates the port, but plans for privatization are under consideration. Tenders for privatization, however, have been pushed back repeatedly. The port at Port-au-Prince occupies nearly 15 hectares and has the service of a gantry crane capable of lifting containers up to 30 tons. Miragoâne and Cap-Haïtien are Haiti's other main ports for exports. Smaller ports at Petit Goâve, Gonaïves, Jacmel, and Port-de-Paix are also active. The county's smaller ports lack the modern machinery needed to handle heavy volume.

Inland Waterways: Haiti has fewer than 100 kilometers of navigable inland waterways. Most of the country's rivers and streams tend to be short and swift flowing because of the mountainous terrain and narrow peninsulas. All the rivers rise and fall significantly with seasons.

Civil Aviation and Airports: Port-au-Prince is home to Haiti's only international airport. Despite poor facilities, the U.S. Department of Transportation examined improvements and declared the airport in fulfillment of international safety standards in 2000. Only two years before, the same body had condemned the airport as unsafe. The small airport at Jérémie serves the domestic travel needs of the southwestern portion of the country. In total, Haiti has four airports with paved runways and eight with unpaved runways. Because of poor facilities at airports, helicopter travel has become an important tool for international forces serving in Haiti.

Pipelines: Haiti has no pipelines.

Telecommunications: Haiti has the lowest telephone density in the Caribbean. Its average of 3.25 subscribers per 100 inhabitants is far below the Latin American/Caribbean average of 34 subscribers per 100 inhabitants. Until recently, the Haitian government completely controlled the telecommunications industry. Most rural people, and many even in urban areas, did not have access to a reliable phone line. Haiti had about 140,000 fixed phone lines in use in 2004. Télécommunications d'Haïti (the state company—Teleco) allowed two new service providers to enter the market in 1998. They made reliable telephone service available to those who could afford it, providing both fixed and mobile wireless phone service. Consequently, the number of cellular subscribers in Haiti increased dramatically—to 400,000 in 2004. Although still expensive for most Haitians, cellular phones have extended phone service into rural areas of the country previously outside the fixed network.

Internet access has come slowly to Haiti. Initially, Teleco refused to give Internet entrepreneurs access to phone lines. However, private companies worked to bring the Internet to the island. The country's first Internet café opened in 1997. In 2003 a U.S. company entered the market to provide broadband Internet service. Later that year, a state plan emerged to subsidize Internet connections for schools. However, the plan was halted before any real progress occurred. As of 2005, Haiti had about 500,000 Internet users. The government does not impose restrictions on Internet access.

GOVERNMENT AND POLITICS

Political System: Haiti's 1987 constitution establishes a semi-presidential system of government that divides power among a president, who serves as chief of state; a prime minister, who serves as head of government; a bicameral legislature (the National Assembly); and regional assemblies.

Haiti traditionally has had a strong presidency. The president serves a five-year term and may not serve consecutive terms. The cabinet, composed of the prime minister and the 15 ministry heads, advises the president, serving at his pleasure. The president shares power with the prime minister, who is nominated by the president and approved by the legislature. The 83-seat Chamber of Deputies and 27-seat Senate form the Haitian legislature, known as the National Assembly. Popularly elected deputies serve four-year terms. Senators serve six-year terms, with one-third of the body being elected every two years. Each department elects three senators. Members of both houses are directly elected and may serve consecutive terms.

The 11-member Supreme Court (or Court of Cassation) operates at the apex of Haiti's judicial system. At the lowest level, justices of the peace issue arrest warrants, adjudicate minor offenses, mediate disputes, and take depositions. Courts of the first instance hear more serious or complicated cases. Appeals from the courts of first instance go before one of the country's 30 appeals courts. The Supreme Court serves as the final arbiter on legal and constitutional questions. A separate court in Port-au-Prince handles labor issues.

Administrative Divisions: Haiti has nine departments: Artibonite, Centre, Grand' Anse, Nord, Nord-Est, Nord-Ouest, Ouest, Sud, and Sud-Est. Before leaving office, President Aristide signed a bill creating a tenth department, but the measure has been awaiting publication since November 2003 and thus has not yet become law.

Provincial and Local Government: Below the federal level, Haiti has a complicated and decentralized system of regional and local governance. Haiti's nine departments are divided into 41 districts, which are further divided into 133 municipalities (called communes). Further dividing the municipalities, 565 communal sections (*sections communales*) exist—roughly equivalent to towns in the United States. Regular elections occur on each level. The communal sections elect a representative council; each of the municipalities elects both a three-member municipal council and a municipal assembly. At the department level, the democratically elected departmental assembly passes legislation, and the departmental council (chosen by the assembly) enforces it.

Judicial and Legal System: Haiti's constitution calls for an independent judiciary to interpret the country's laws, which are based on the Napoleonic Code. The criminal code dates to 1832, although some amendments have been made. The constitution guarantees defendants the right to a fair public trial, including the presumption of innocence and the right to be present at trial, to present witnesses and evidence in their own defense, and to confront witnesses against them. In practice, however these rights are often denied. Moreover, the government is not required to provide free counsel, and many Haitians cannot afford representation on their own. The judiciary, like most of the government, suffers from widespread corruption. Threats of violence often render judges and juries unable to make impartial decisions. Bribes not only sway judges but also taint potential witnesses. In addition to corruption, the judicial system suffers from shortages of both funding and qualified personnel. The combination of corruption and inefficiency has resulted in a serious backlog of criminal cases and an overflow in the country's jails. Nearly 80 percent of incarcerated men and women still await their initial trail, despite some effort in 2005 to reduce pretrial detention.

Electoral System: All Haitians 18 years of age or older have the right to vote. According to the constitution, elections should occur in Haiti at least every two years, to fill the presidency, legislature, or local offices. Violence, however, has made this schedule impossible since 2004 and at previous times in Haiti's history. Presidential elections are to be held every five years, but few presidents have reached the end of their terms. Coups frequently have upset the electoral schedule. Elections to choose a new president and parliament were held in Feburary 2006.

Electoral law requires that legislative candidates receive more than 50 percent of the vote in order to win office during the first round of elections. If no candidate for a seat wins more than

50 percent, a run-off election occurs. Haiti's Provisional Electoral Council (Conseil Electoral Provisoire—CEP) oversees all electoral activities. Although nominally independent, the CEP is routinely subjected to political manipulation by the party in power. During the February 2006 elections, the CEP was widely criticized for its initial decision to count an unusually large number of blank ballots, which would have denied René Préval the majority needed for a first-round victory. Facing international criticism and domestic protests, the CEP later reversed itself and declared Préval the first-round winner. The second round of the parliamentary elections was held on April 21, 2006, without incident.

Politics and Political Parties: Numerous political parties—most of them small—field candidates in elections. Some parties aspire to have broad influence but are unwilling to bend from their single-issue focus. Others exist merely as fronts for ambitious individuals. The smaller Haitian political parties often form alliances and coalitions. President Aristide's Lavalas Family (Fanmi Lavalas—FL) party continues to receive a large measure of support. A broad alliance of democratically minded parties known as the Democratic Convergence (Convergence Démocratique—CD) provides the most distinguishable opposition to FL. Other umbrella coalitions attempting to unite smaller parties include the Alliance for the Liberation and Advancement of Haiti (ALAH), Grand Center Right Front Coalition, and Haitian Greater Socialist Party (Grand Parti Socialiste Haïtien—GPSH).

Although the army disbanded in 1995, former military personnel remain a political force. Many former officers participated in the opposition movement that led to President Aristide's ouster. Similarly, the Roman Catholic Church continues to exert influence on the political scene. During the Duvalier dictatorship of the 1980s, political parties and trade unions were crushed, leaving only the Catholic Church to represent the interests of those oppressed by the government. Since that time, the church has become less political but remains a potential political advocate for opposition groups.

Mass Media: As in many developing countries, radio reaches the widest audience in Haiti. Estimates vary, but more than 300 radio stations are believed to broadcast throughout the country. Talk show programs serve as one of the few ways in which ordinary Haitians can speak out about politics and the government. A law passed in 1997 declares the airwaves to be the property of the government, but at least 133 unlicensed radio stations operate freely. In addition, there are 50 community-based stations throughout the country.

Television is available only to a minority of relatively wealthy households. Two television stations serve approximately 42,000 households that have television receivers. Satellite stations from foreign countries are available in Haiti, but only to those with the expensive equipment necessary to receive them. Haiti's three French-language newspapers have a total circulation of less than 20,000. Small, Creole-language newspapers are printed irregularly.

Foreign Relations: Multinational organizations have long played a role in Haiti's development. Presently, United Nations (UN) peacekeeping troops operate in Haiti. In 2004 the UN Security Council authorized the UN Stabilization Mission in Haiti (MINUSTAH), which provided troops and police personnel to Haiti for an extended duration. Additionally, the World Bank and

International Monetary Fund have funded many improvements in Haiti's economic infrastructure, education system, and health care network.

In large part as a result of its proximity, the United States has shown a prolonged interest in creating economic stability and functional democracy in Haiti. During the U.S. occupation of Haiti (1915–34), U.S. Marines developed many laws and practices that still exist in the country. The United States serves as Haiti's primary partner for both exports and imports and, in 1994, took an active role in restoring President Aristide to power. In 2000 President Bill Clinton signed legislation suspending economic aid to Haiti based on U.S. government concerns over the legitimacy of parliamentary elections and an absence of accountability practices. Most U.S. and international aid was restored in July 2004.

Haiti's ties to its neighbors grew stronger during the 1990s. Relations with the Dominican Republic, which traditionally had been strained by border disputes and the perception that the Dominican police mistreat Haitian workers in the Dominican Republic, improved. A visit by President René Préval (1996–2000) to the Dominican Republic in 1996 was followed by a meeting between President Aristide (2000–4) and the Dominican president, Hipólito Mejía, in 2002. The countries agreed on a "free-trade zone" to provide jobs for Haitians and labor for Dominican companies.

Since 2000, trade has increased among all Caribbean countries. In 2002 the Dominican Republic was second only to the United States in trade with Haiti. Additionally, Haiti conducted significant trade with Trinidad and Tobago. In another significant step, Haiti achieved full membership in the Caribbean Community and Common Market (Caricom) in 2002. However, after President Aristide fled Haiti in 2004, Caricom refused to recognize Haiti's interim government because of concerns that Aristide may have been pressured to resign through antidemocratic means. Some Caricom member states began normalizing relations with the interim administration of President Boniface Alexandre during 2005, and the organization welcomed the new Préval administration.

Membership in International Organizations: Haiti was an original member of the United Nations (UN). Haiti maintains that membership and supports many of the UN's specialized agencies. Haiti also belongs to the International Labour Organization, International Monetary Fund, International Organization for Migration, World Health Organization, and World Trade Organization. Regionally, Haiti has membership in the African, Caribbean, and Pacific Group of States (ACP Group), Inter-American Development Bank, Latin American Economic System, and Organization of American States (OAS). Haiti's membership in the Caribbean Community and Common Market (Caricom) was suspended following Aristide's resignation in 2004. Some Caricom members reestablished relations with Haiti, but the organization withheld full recognition until elections were held in February 2006.

Major International Treaties: Haiti is a party to many significant treaties, including international agreements on agriculture, customs, genocide, human rights, intellectual property, labor, and nuclear non-proliferation. Haiti is a signatory to numerous environmental agreements, including those on biodiversity, climate change, desertification, law of the sea, marine dumping, marine life conservation, and ozone layer protection. Treaties to which Haiti has withheld support include agreements on biological weapons, chemical weapons, conservation, and gas warfare.

NATIONAL SECURITY

Armed Forces Overview: After years of military interference in politics, including dozens of military coups, Haiti disbanded its military in 1995. Haiti's National Assembly created a new civilian police with the help of the United States and the United Nations. Yet, to date there has been no official constitutional amendment to abolish the military. The UN Stabilization Mission in Haiti (MINUSTAH) has been authorized to complete the disarmament and demobilization of any remaining militias.

Foreign Military Relations: Without its own military, Haiti relies heavily on United Nations (UN) peacekeeping forces. The multinational force has been responsible for quelling riots and preparing for democratic elections. Before UN forces arrived, a multilateral force made up of troops from Canada, Chile, France, and the United States helped stabilize the country under the interim leadership of President Boniface Alexandre.

External Threat: Haiti has no obvious external threats. Tensions have long existed between Haiti and the Dominican Republic, but the current border has been fixed since 1936.

Defense Budget: In 2003 Haiti's civilian security budget totaled an estimated US$26 million.

Major Military Units: None.

Major Military Equipment: None.

Military Service: None.

Paramilitary Forces: None.

Foreign Military Forces: In June 2005, the United Nations Security Council authorized a reinforcement of the UN Stabilization Mission in Haiti (MINUSTAH)—from 6,700 troops and 1,600 civilian police to 7,500 troops and 1,900 civilian police—to provide security during the run-up to national elections in February 2006. On June 6, 2005, the UN military force launched a coordinated series of operations against armed gangs in Port-au-Prince. By February 2006, 21 nations had contributed military personnel, and 31 nations had contributed police personnel to MINUSTAH. Brazil was the largest single contributor of military personnel with 1,200 troops. From February to May 2005, the U.S. Southern Command carried out a humanitarian mission in Haiti entitled "New Horizons 2005." The task force built schools, drilled wells, provided preventative health services, and set up temporary housing for orphaned children. Troops from all branches of the U.S. armed forces participated.

Military Forces Abroad: None.

Police: Other than the temporary United Nations Stabilization Mission in Haiti (MINUSTAH) force, the Haitian National Police (Police Nationale d'Haïti—PNH) is the only security force in the country following the disbandment of the Haitian military. According to the U.S. Department of State, the PNP is an "officially autonomous" civilian force headed by a director general whose activities are overseen by the minister of justice and the secretary of state for public security within the Ministry of Justice. The PNH has an estimated 2,000 personnel. Specialized units are dedicated to crime response (SWAT), crowd control in Port-au-Prince, security in the Ouest Department, and presidential security. Although officially part of the police force, the Presidential Security Unit operates with its own budget and administration.

During President Aristide's second term (2000–4) political appointees took over many key positions in the PNH. In many instances, these appointees lacked security experience and compromised the political neutrality of the force. After Aristide fled the country, the interim president removed 200 corrupt and inexperienced officers in an effort to improve the PNH's effectiveness. New training ensued to teach police officers how to balance security and human rights concerns. However, numerous problems limit the PNH's effectiveness and reliability. Former military personnel exert considerable influence within the police force, and some have begun to push for the reestablishment of the Haitian army.

Since its inception, the PNH has suffered from mismanagement, corruption, and a lack of funding. MINUSTAH has helped make up for the shortfalls of the PNH since it arrived in Haiti in 2004. Many security operations have been undertaken jointly by the PNH and MINUSTAH. Nevertheless, rampant crime and gang violence continue to be the most immediate problem facing Haitian authorities.

Internal Threat: Crime and militant activity are the most serious internal threats in Haiti. Security forces focus on these issues rather than on external threats. Amnesty International reports that the efforts of the United Nations (UN) and Haiti's police force have largely failed to curb violent crime in the country, especially in the capital region. The organization estimates that, in Port-au-Prince, an average of 100 persons per month were murdered in 2004. Amnesty International asserts that perpetrators act with virtual impunity because the police and courts are corrupt and ineffective. The U.S. Department of State has issued numerous travel advisories warning U.S. citizens of the potential for looting, blockades by armed gangs, and violent crime including kidnapping, carjacking, and assault. The U.S. embassy in Port-au-Prince frequently has imposed a 5 p.m. curfew on its employees.

In addition to isolated incidents of violent crime, Haiti has a large organized crime network. Former members of the armed forces have formed armed brigades and claim that the government owes them remuneration for their role in ousting President Aristide. Drug traffickers also operate in the country. Haiti has become a major transit point for cocaine entering the United States and Europe. Officials in the United States estimate that 8 percent of the cocaine entering the United States travels through Haiti. Additionally, a legacy of political corruption and tainted elections has led to a pattern of violent political protest.

Terrorism: Haiti has no known terrorist groups operating within its borders. Although violence and crime are rampant, there have been no reported terrorist attacks in Haiti. The U.S.

ambassador to Haiti has called the political violence in the country the work of "terrorists" but only in reference to strongmen carrying out violence with the approval of Haitian politicians.

Human Rights: According to its constitution and written laws, Haiti meets most international human rights standards. In practice, however, many provisions are not observed. The government's human rights record is poor. Arbitrary and political killings, kidnapping, disappearances, torture, and unlawful arrest and incarceration are common unofficial practices, especially during periods of coups or attempted coups. Prisons are overcrowded and unsanitary. Although the constitution mandates an independent judiciary and the right to a fair trial, prolonged pretrial detention remains a serious problem. Because the court system and its records are poorly organized, it is impossible to determine the percentage of prisoners being held without trial.

The constitution guarantees freedom of speech and of the press, and the government generally has respected these rights. Many journalists, however, practice a measure of self-censorship in order to protect themselves from retribution. During the second Aristide administration (2000–4), some reports contend that members of the press were killed for supporting opposition movements. The government does not censor radio, television, or the Internet. Security forces frequently have ignored the constitutionally mandated right to assembly and organization. The Haitian government generally has respected religious freedom in the country.

Haiti's constitution does not contain specific language prohibiting discrimination on the basis of race, sex, language, age, or disability. Although some working standards are intended to protect women, few resources exist to ensure enforcement. Abuses against women and children are common. Rape, although illegal, rarely results in prosecution of the perpetrator. Haitian law excuses a husband for murdering his wife if the wife is found in an adulterous affair. The Haitian government contains a Ministry of Women's Affairs but lacks the resources to address issues such as violence against women and harassment in the workplace. In addition to suffering from chronic malnourishment and a lack of educational opportunity, many Haitian children also suffer physical abuse. Few statistics regarding the wider problem of child abuse have been collected. Trafficking of children also is a significant problem. The United Nations Children's Fund (UNICEF) estimates that 2,000 to 3,000 Haitian children per year are trafficked to the Dominican Republic.